T0050888

10-MINUTE PROJECTS

65 Projects You Can Make in a Flash

BY SARAH L. SCHUETTE

CAPSTONE PRESS
a capstone imprint

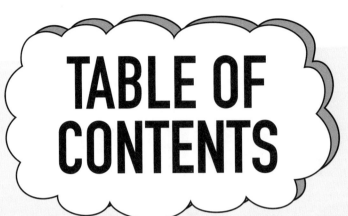

TABLE OF CONTENTS

GOT 1⏱ MINUTES?

You may be running short on time,
but that doesn't mean you can't
whip up some fun!

These quick and easy projects will inspire you. Ask an adult to help you, grab some supplies, and then get making!

GENERAL SUPPLIES AND TOOLS

baking soda

bowls, jars, or plastic containers

cardboard

card stock

clothespins

cornstarch

craft sticks

crayons

dough or clay

dry-erase marker

duct tape, different colors
 and patterns

felt or craft foam

flour

food coloring

glue or tape

magazines

markers and pens

notebook

paper and pencil

paint

paper clips

paper plates

plastic cutting board/mat

rotary cutting tool
  or pizza cutter

rubber bands

ruler

salt

scissors or
  craft knife

shaving cream

straws

vinegar

washi tape

water

yarn or string

TIPS

- Before starting a project, gather the supplies and tools needed.

- Ask an adult to help you with sharp tools.

- Use a toolbox to hold your building supplies. You can build on the go and stay organized.

- Wear an old shirt or apron to keep your clothes clean.

- Wear plastic gloves and safety goggles when doing science experiments.

- Dry-erase markers work great for tracing or drawing on duct tape. Just wipe away the marks if you don't want them to show.

- When making a long project with duct tape, cut shorter strips and tape them together. Long single strips of tape can be tough to handle.

- To make clean cuts on duct tape, stick the tape to a plastic mat. Use a rotary cutting tool to cut the strips. Peel the tape up from the board and add it to your project. If the piece of tape is too short, just stick a new piece on it.

- Change things up! Don't be afraid to make these projects your own.

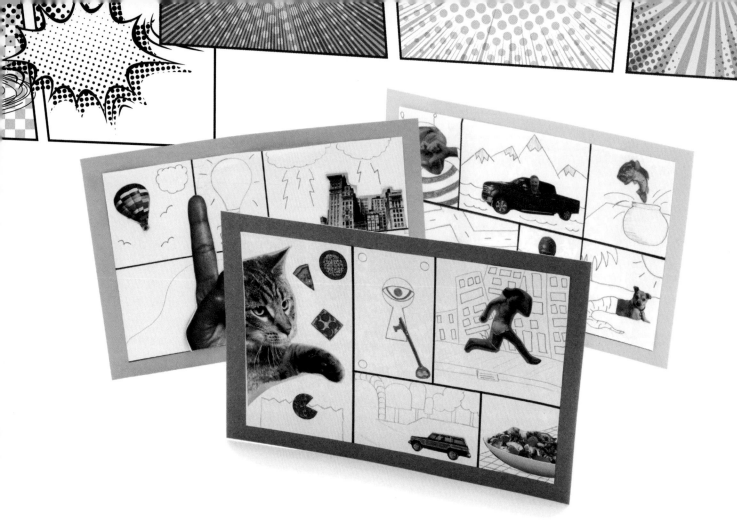

GRAPHIC ART MASTERPIECE

Artists often mix materials to make their creations. Combine your drawings and story-writing abilities with pictures you find in magazines. Tell your own story!

What You Need:

magazines

old books

scissors

ruler

marker

paper or notebook

glue

pencil

What You Do:

1 Gather magazines, old books, or anything with pictures that you can cut out.

2 Draw grids on a piece of paper with a ruler and marker.

3 Glue one picture in each grid.

4 Draw bodies or scenes around the pictures with the pencil.

TIP Glue your art into a notebook or journal. Write a story to go with your funny pictures.

WHO ARE YOU?

Artists express how they see themselves by making self-portraits or sculptures. How do you see yourself? How do you see others? Express yourself!

What You Need:

phone or tablet camera

pencil

2 pieces of card stock,
  8½x11 inches
  (22x28 centimeters)

scissors

What You Do:

1 Ask a friend to take a close-up picture of the profile of your face. Look closely at the image. Draw your profile on the card stock and then cut it out.

2 Ask a friend to take a close-up picture of you facing the camera. Look closely at the image. On a second piece of card stock, draw the outline of your head and shoulders. Cut it out.

3 Cut a slit down from the top of the head on the side profile piece. On the other outline, cut a slit up from the bottom center.

4 Slide the two pieces together so they stand up.

TIP Do this project with a friend. Put your faces together to make a friendship sculpture.

15

SCOPE IT OUT

A basic color wheel builds colors
from red, yellow, and blue. See how light
transforms these primary colors
in this eye-catching kaleidoscope.

What You Need:

- cardboard tube
- clear plastic or chip can lids
- marker
- scissors
- hot glue or tape
- beads or tissue paper
- craft stick
- card stock
- foil
- craft paper and washi tape

What You Do:

1 Set the tube on the plastic and trace it twice with a marker. Cut out the plastic circles. They should be a bit smaller than the tube. Glue or tape one circle in the end of the tube.

2 Drop colorful plastic beads or pieces of tissue paper into the tube. Use a craft stick to push the second plastic circle into the tube. It should rest on top of the beads and tissue.

3 Fold a piece of card stock in thirds to make a triangle. Cover it with foil and tape. Slide the foil triangle inside the tube. Trim the triangle if it sticks out of the tube's end.

4 Decorate your kaleidoscope with craft paper and washi tape.

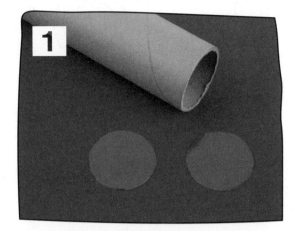

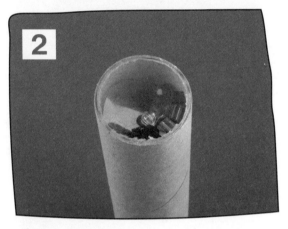

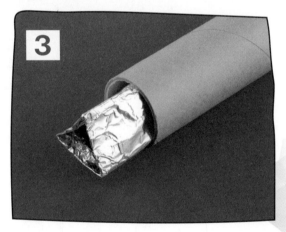

TIP Point your kaleidoscope at a window or a light and look through it. Turn the tube to see the different shapes and colors mix together.

CUBE IT!

Art often plays with texture, shape, color, and form.
What elements will you mix together? Use what you
have available. The possibilities are endless!

What You Need:

pencil

ruler

paper or card stock

scissors

markers

washi tape, scrap paper, buttons

What You Do:

1 Draw a hexagon on a piece of paper. Cut it out.

2 Draw three lines on the hexagon to make it look like a cube.

3 Decorate the cube with washi tape, scrap paper, buttons, or any art supplies you have available.

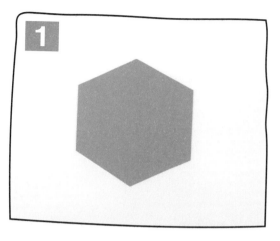

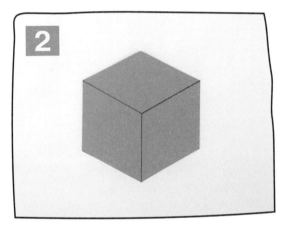

TIP Make any shape you can imagine using this technique. How can you add different textures?

UNICORN DUST

Practice your color-mixing skills
and create unicorn dust! Use it to decorate
a fairy garden or layer it in a tiny jar necklace.
You can even paint with it!

What You Need:

salt, ¼ cup (57 grams)
   per color

measuring cup

zip-top bags

food coloring

small bottle

yarn or string

What You Do:

1   Pour salt into a zip-top bag.

2   Add one drop of food coloring to the salt. Zip the bag closed.

3   Kneed the bag until all of the salt is colored.

4   Repeat steps 1–3 to make more colors. Add more drops to make the colors brighter.

5   Pour layers of colorful salt into a tiny bottle or clear container.

TIP Tie a piece of yarn or string around the bottle's neck to make a necklace.

21

KINDNESS ROCKS!

Being kind makes everyone feel good! Leave these cute rocks as little surprises for friends who have shown you kindness.

What You Need:

- rocks
- yarn
- paint
- markers
- glue
- googly eyes or felt (optional)

What You Do:

1 Drizzle glue on a rock and wrap the rock in yarn. Or paint a face on it.

2 Add other details with stickers, scrap paper, or patterned tape.

TIP Add googly eyes or felt to create even more fun looks with your rocks.

LEAF LOVE

Use what you find in nature to make art! Our world
is full of beautiful things. Take a look around
and see what inspires you!

What You Need:

leaves, sticks, or anything
    you collect in nature

scissors

card stock

craft paper

glue

What You Do:

1 Go outside! Gather leaves, pine cones, seeds, or anything that is beautiful to you.

2 Cut pieces of card stock to fit each leaf. Glue the leaves onto the paper.

3 Use craft paper to add frames to the card stock pieces.

TIP Hang your creations in your room or give them to friends as gifts.

25

SQUISHY GARDEN

Turn old, mismatched socks into an art project.
Fill them with dough and plant your own
squishy sock garden.

What You Need:

old socks

dough, clay, or flour

scissors

felt or craft foam

googly eyes or marker

paper or plastic containers

What You Do:

1 Fill each sock with dough. Tie the opening of each sock in a knot.

2 Squish the dough to make a fruit, vegetable, or any shape you wish.

3 Cut out leaves and stems from felt or foam. Glue them to the socks.

4 Add googly eyes or draw faces with a marker.

5 "Plant" your socks in containers.

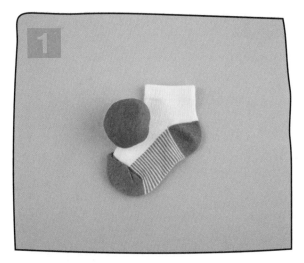

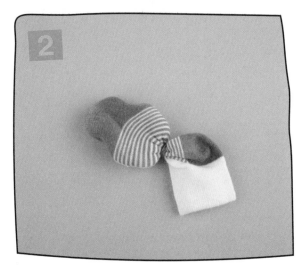

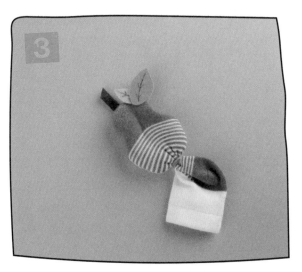

TIP If you don't have old socks, fill balloons with dough or flour instead. You can also add colorful sand or salt as "dirt" if you like.

BOTTLE CAP MAGNETS

The options are endless with these simple little magnets. What will you make?

What You Need:

bottle caps of different sizes

glue

craft magnets

felt, googly eyes, yarn,
    washi tape, or craft paper

string (optional)

What You Do:

1 Glue a metal bottle cap to the inside of a plastic bottle cap.

2 Glue a craft magnet on the back.

3 Decorate with felt, googly eyes, yarn, washi tape, or paper shapes.

1

2

TIP Instead of stacking bottle caps, simply decorate one however you'd like. Be creative and have fun!

EMOJI PINS (NOSE-OJIS)

Create your own emoji-inspired pins!
Introducing, NOSE-OJIS. These funny faces
with silly noses are sure to make you smile.

What You Need:

paper or plastic cup

felt or craft foam

marker

scissors

glue

mini clothespins
   or safety pins

What You Do:

1 Set a cup on a piece of felt or foam. Trace around the bottom of the cup. Cut out the circle. Repeat this for as many pins as you'd like.

2 Draw noses and other facial features on other pieces of felt or foam. Cut them out.

3 Glue the face pieces to the circles.

4 Glue clothespins or safety pins to the backs of the circles.

TIP Make animal nose-ojis!

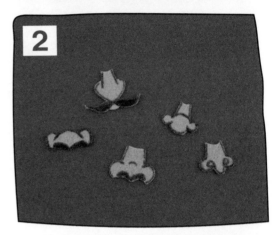

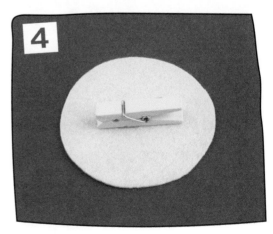

SHADOW ART PUZZLES

Artists often play with shadows and light. Challenge
yourself with this puzzle created
with shadows and light. Can you put it
back together correctly?

What You Need:

10 craft sticks

tape

toy

flashlight

markers and paint

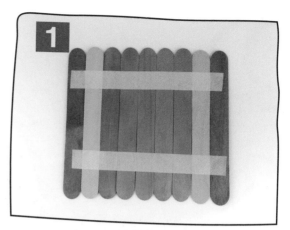

What You Do:

1 Lay 10 craft sticks next to each other. Tape them together.

2 Stand the craft sticks up against a wall or a book, tape side facing the back.

3 Set the toy in front of the sticks and shine a flashlight at it. Adjust the light so it makes a shadow of the toy on the sticks.

4 Trace the shadow on the sticks with a marker.

5 Paint or decorate the sticks. Remove the tape.

6 Mix up the sticks and put the puzzle back together.

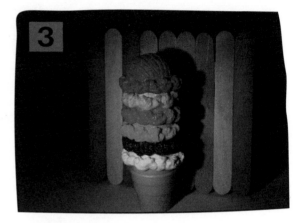

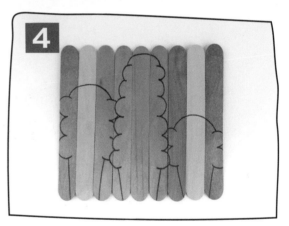

TIP Instead of a toy, mold clay or foil into any shape you wish. Try making a puzzle with different shadows put together. Be creative!

PICASSO BOT

Express your love of all things technical by making your own robot! Turn a recycled can into a holder for your art supplies.

What You Need:

marker

craft stick

craft paper

soup can or coffee can

glue

bottle cap
  and magnet

pipe cleaners

yarn

What You Do:

1 Draw lines on a craft stick to look like teeth. Wrap the paper around the can. Then glue the stick to the paper.

2 Stick a bottle cap to the can with a magnet to make an eye.

3 Coil pipe cleaners around your finger. Glue them to the sides of the can to look like arms.

4 Use leftover yarn pieces to make hair.

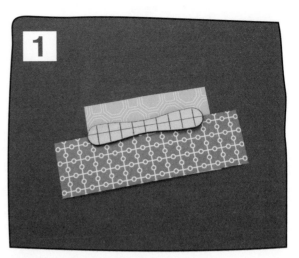

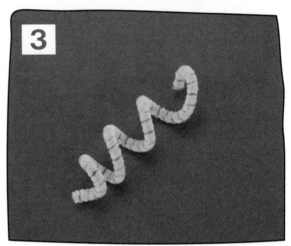

TIP Store your extra art supplies in your robot.

GEOMETRIC STACKERS

Shapes are an important part of making art.
These geometric stackers will showcase
colorful shapes as art.

What You Need:

scissors

cardboard or craft foam

markers or paint

What You Do:

1 Cut circles, squares, or triangles out of cardboard or craft foam. The shapes can all be the same size, or they can be different.

2 Decorate cardboard shapes with markers or paint.

3 Cut slits around the edges of the shapes. Stack them together!

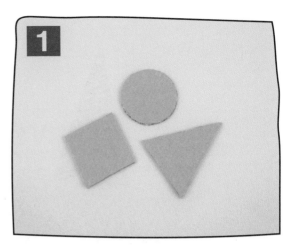

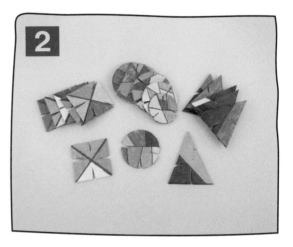

TIP Ask your friends to make more shapes. Work together to see how high you can stack them!

SQUISHY PAL

Have you ever wanted to create your own stuffed animal? Now is your chance! This squishy pal makes the perfect playmate.

What You Need:

5 duct tape strips, about
   10 inches (25 cm) long

cutting board

scissors

cotton balls, old socks,
   or anything squishy

additional duct tape

What You Do:

1 Stick one strip of duct tape to a cutting board. Add a second strip on top, overlapping the long edge by ¼ inch (0.64 cm). Repeat with two more strips of tape, but with sticky parts facing up. You will have two large tape rectangles.

2 Place one large rectangle on top of the other, sticky sides together.

3 Fold the rectangle in half widthwise to make a pouch.

4 Cut the remaining strip of duct tape in half widthwise. Use it to tape the sides of the pouch shut.

5 Stuff the pouch with cotton balls or old socks. Tape the top of the pouch shut.

6 Use more duct tape to add a horn, eyes, or any features you like.

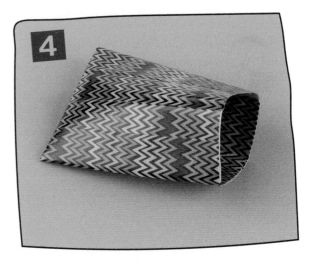

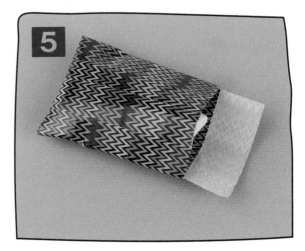

TIP Skip the stuffing and leave the pouch open. Add a duct tape strap to make a bag.

FEATHER BACKPACK PULL

Jazz up your backpack zipper with a cute feather. You can easily make this into earrings, a necklace, or a pin too.

What You Need:

1 duct tape strip, about 8 inches (20 cm) long

dry-erase marker

scissors or rotary cutting tool

awl (optional)

metal clasp or ring/paper clip

What You Do:

1 Fold the duct tape strip in half widthwise, sticky sides together.

2 Draw a feather or raindrop shape on the front of the tape with the dry-erase marker.

3 Cut out the shape. Then make small cuts along the edges to create fringe.

4 Poke a hole in the top of the feather with scissors or an awl.

5 Slide a metal clasp, ring, or paper clip through the hole. Attach to your backpack zipper.

TIP Try using a pizza cutter or any rotary cutting tool to make exact cuts in your duct tape creations.

BEAUTIFUL BEADS

Want to decorate your wrist? Twirl a bunch
of duct tape beads and string them together to
make a funky bracelet. Then show your friends
your new jewelry!

What You Need:

4 duct tape strips, about
½ inch (1.3 cm) wide

scissors

paper straw

yarn or string, long enough
to wrap around your wrist

additional duct tape
in different colors

plastic beads, feathers,
or charms (optional)

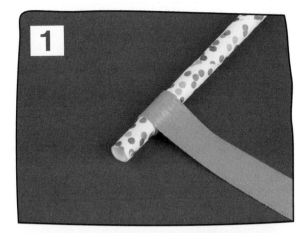

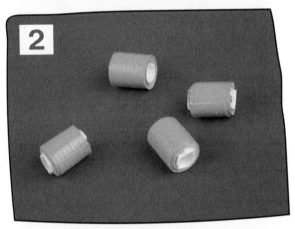

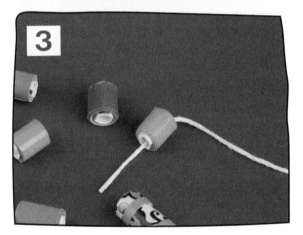

What You Do:

1 Stick each duct tape strip to a paper straw. Roll the straws to make bead shapes with the tape.

2 Cut the straw at each side of every bead. The straw shouldn't stick out past the ends of the tape beads.

3 Thread the yarn or string through the beads.

4 Repeat steps 1–2 to make more beads and build your bracelet. Change the size of the tape strips to make longer or thicker beads. Add thinner strips of tape on top of the beads to add a second color.

5 Tie a knot to end the bracelet.

TIP Team up with friends and make friendship bracelets for each other. Add in plastic beads, feathers, or charms!

GIANT LETTER TILE

Pick a letter and create a tile. Work together with friends to create a meaningful word to display at home or school.

What You Need:

1 cardboard square, about 8x8 inches (20x20 cm)

duct tape, 3 colors

ruler

cutting board

dry-erase marker

scissors

What You Do:

1 Wrap a cardboard square in one color of duct tape. Wrap the edges with a second color of tape.

2 Stick a 3½-inch (8.9 cm) piece of duct tape to a cutting board. Draw a letter on top with a dry-erase marker.

3 Cut out the letter and stick it to the middle of the square.

4 Work with friends to spell out a colorful word to display at school or home.

DESK
STATION

Design your own desk station! Jot down important
reminders or show off your latest drawings in style.
Plus, store all your stuff in these cute containers.

What You Need:

1 cardboard square, about 8x8 inches (20x20 cm)

scissors

dry-erase sheet or tape

cardboard box and cardboard tube

duct tape

dry-erase markers

What You Do:

1 Wrap the cardboard square in a sticky dry-erase sheet or tape.

2 Wrap a small cardboard box and cardboard tube in duct tape. Make sure to cover one end of the tube with tape.

3 Stick the box and tube to the cardboard square with more duct tape.

4 Use more duct tape to decorate the board. Be creative!

TIP This handy desk station can be turned into a locker station. Just stick it to your locker door with more duct tape!

PICTURE PROP

Do you like taking pictures and selfies?
Get goofy and create a silly prop for your pics!

What You Need:

1 duct tape strip, about
  12 inches (25 cm) long

dry-erase marker

scissors or rotary cutting tool

additional duct tape

craft stick

digital camera or phone camera

What You Do:

1 Fold the duct tape strip in half widthwise, sticky sides together.

2 Draw a bow tie, glasses, or other fun shape on the duct tape with the marker.

3 Cut out the shape.

4 Tape the shape to a craft stick.

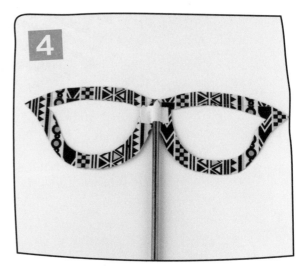

TIP Work together with friends to create a bunch of fun props. Make your own photo booth by hanging a colorful sheet on a wall or in a doorway. Then start snapping your goofy pics with those props!

PROP BOX WITH BOW

Now that you have props for your photos, make a duct tape box to store them in. You'll smile every time you unpack the box. You can even make your own bow!

What You Need:

3 duct tape strips, about
    8 inches (20 cm) long

additional duct tape

1 duct tape strip, about
    4 inches (10 cm) long

cardboard box, about
    16x13 inches (41x33 cm)

What You Do:

1 Fold all three 8-inch (20-cm) strips of duct tape in half lengthwise, sticky sides together.

2 Fold each strip so the ends meet in the middle. Tape the ends down.

3 Set the pieces on top of each other and fan them out like a bow. Tape the strips where they meet in the middle.

4 Fold the 4-inch (10-cm) tape strip in half lengthwise, sticky sides together. Then fold it together as you did in Step 2. Tape it on top of the bow.

5 Decorate a cardboard box with duct tape and add the bow on top.

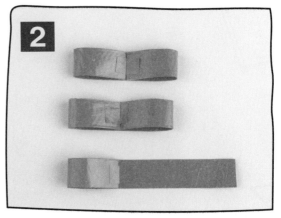

TIP This beautiful box can be used for gift-giving too!

MAGIC
WALLET

Amaze your friends with this tricky wallet.
The money inside will magically change places!

What You Need:

2 pieces of cardboard, about 3x5 inches (7.6x13 cm)

2 duct tape strips, about 10 inches (25 cm) long

additional duct tape

scissors or rotary cutting tool

What You Do:

1 Cover both sides of each piece of cardboard with duct tape.

2 Fold each duct tape strip in half lengthwise. Cut each strip in half to make four pieces.

3 Use two strips to make an X in the center of one cardboard piece. Place a third strip above the X. Place the last strip below the X.

4 Set the second cardboard piece on top of the strips. On the left side, tape the ends of the top and bottom strips to the cardboard.

5 On the right side, tape the ends of the X to the cardboard.

6 Flip over the whole thing. Then stick the remaining tape ends to the cardboard.

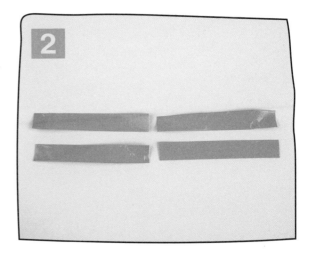

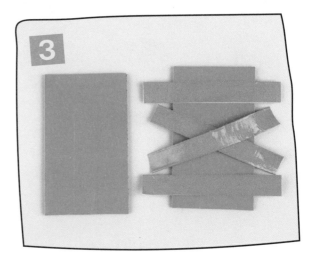

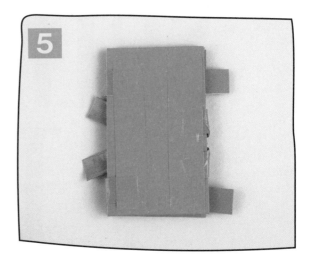

TIP Slide a dollar bill between the two parallel strips. Flip the wallet back and forth. You'll be amazed at how the money inside moves from side to side.

SPINNING TOP

Keep your hands busy with this simple
spinning top. Give your top a twirl
and see how long it spins!

What You Need:

pencil

duct tape

cardboard

scissors

1 wooden dowel, about
2½ inches (6.4 cm) long

bead with large hole

What You Do:

1 Trace the inside of a roll of duct tape onto cardboard. Cut out the circle and cover with duct tape.

2 Slide one end of the dowel into the hole in the bead. Wrap the other end of the dowel with tape.

3 Cut an X in the center of the cardboard circle. The X should be just big enough to hold the bead. Push the bead, with the stick pointing up, through the hole. The bead should poke out on each side of the circle.

4 Twist the stick and let it go. Watch the spinner spin!

DECAL CRAZY!

Decorate your school supplies with duct tape. Make your pencils, notebooks, and bulletin boards unique with your own duct tape decals.

What You Need:

duct tape

wax paper or parchment paper

marker

scissors or rotary cutting tool

What You Do:

1. Stick duct tape to a piece of wax paper.

2. Flip the wax paper over. Then draw a shape where the duct tape is.

3. Cut out the shape. Then peel the wax paper off the shape.

4. Stick the decal wherever you'd like!

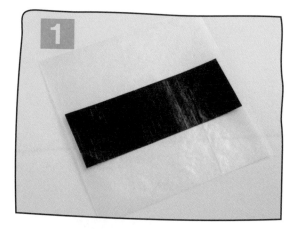

BOOKMARK

Mark your spot in style! This quick and easy bookmark will make reading even more fun.

What You Need:

1 piece of card stock,
2x5 inches (5.1x13 cm)

1 duct tape strip, about
10 inches (25 cm) long

hole punch

ribbon

additional duct tape

What You Do:

1 Lay the piece of card stock over half of the sticky side of the piece of duct tape.

2 Fold the tape to cover the other side of the card stock.

3 Punch a hole in one end of the bookmark.

4 Tie a piece of ribbon through the hole.

5 Decorate the bookmark with smaller strips of duct tape.

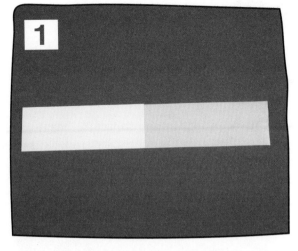

TABLET HOLDER

Keep your tech gear safe and secure
with a tablet holder that's totally your style.

What You Need:

one piece of card stock,
   8.5x11 inches (22x28 cm)

duct tape, different colors

2 duct tape strips, about
   8 inches (20 cm) long

1 duct tape strip, about 4 inches
   (10 cm) long

hook-and-loop fasteners

What You Do:

1 Cover both sides of the card stock with duct tape.

2 Fold the covered card stock in half.

3 Stick one 8-inch (20-cm) strip of duct tape to a cutting board. Add the second strip, overlapping the long edge by ¼ inch (0.6 cm). Then fold it, sticky parts together. This piece will be a pocket.

4 Attach the pocket to the inside bottom corner of the holder with extra pieces of tape.

5 Fold the 4-inch (10-cm) strip in half, lengthwise. Tape half of the strip to the back cover.

6 Remove the backing from the fastener. Add one side of it to the sticky end of the tape strip. Stick the other part of the fastener to the front cover, where it will meet up with the first part.

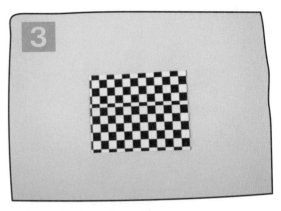

TIP Use the strap to keep the tablet holder closed when you aren't using it.

PENCIL TOPPER

Add some flair to your writing tool with a duct tape flower! Challenge yourself to make different sizes, shapes, and color combinations.

What You Need:

2 duct tape strips, about 12 inches (30 cm) long

scissors

pencil

What You Do:

1. Lay one piece of duct tape sticky side up. Lay the other piece on top, sticky side down, leaving ¼ inch (0.6 cm) of the sticky part showing on each strip.

2. Fold the tape over to make a tube opening. Then stick it down on itself.

3. Cut small slits along the folded side of the tape tube. Do not cut all the way through.

4. Stick the tape, slit side out, to the eraser end of a pencil. Wrap the tape around the eraser to make a bow or flower. Use extra tape to secure it to the pencil.

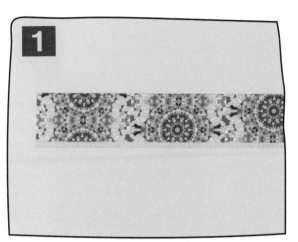

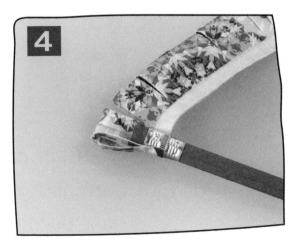

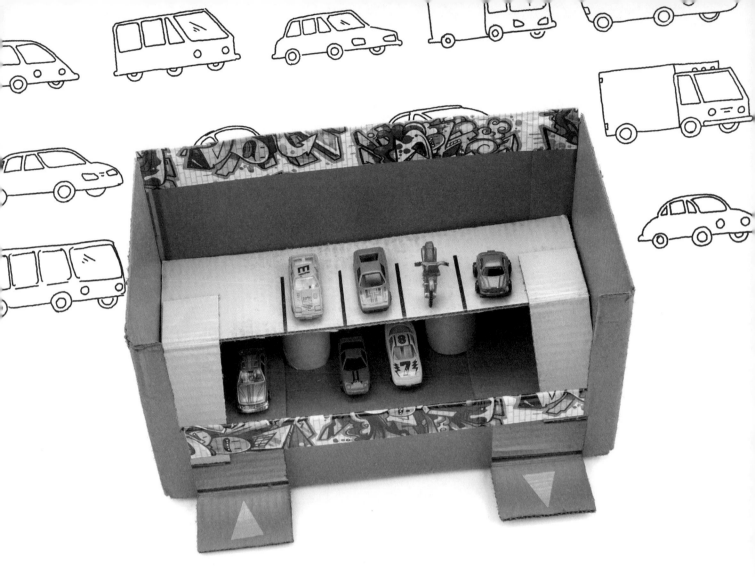

PARKING GARAGE

Engineers design and build things all around us.
You can think like an engineer too! Try designing
and building a parking garage.

What You Need:

cardboard box

scissors or craft knife

paper-towel tube

duct tape

pencils, pens, markers,
    paint, or crayons

What You Do:

1 Cut the flaps off a cardboard box.

2 Cut two holes in the front of the box to make an entrance and exit. Also cut off the top front of the box.

3 Cut two pieces, each 2.5 inches (6.4 cm) long, from a paper-towel tube. Set the pieces inside the box as support pillars.

4 Use the cardboard flaps to make ramps. Set them on top of the tube pieces. Duct tape the pieces together.

5 Decorate the garage with paint, markers, and duct tape.

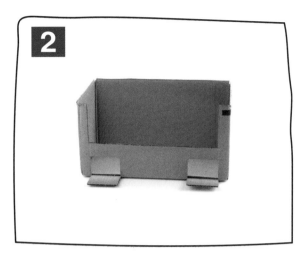

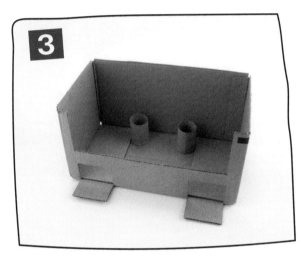

65

BUILDING BLOCK PUZZLE

Engineers often have to solve problems or puzzles
to help make a design work. Are you a puzzler?
Find out with these fun polyomino puzzles!

What You Need:

foam cubes (at least 20)

glue

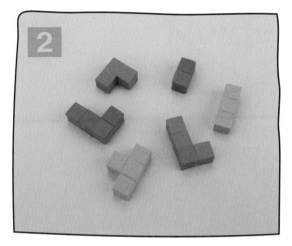

What You Do:

1 Sort the cubes into groups of 2, 3, and 4.

2 Glue the cubes together to make different shapes.

3 Place the cube shapes together like puzzle pieces. Create one large rectangle or another fun shape.

4 Take the puzzle apart and make new shapes.

TIP Before gluing your foam cubes together, try rearranging them on a flat surface to create the puzzle you want. Once you know the shape, glue the cubes together.

JUMPING JACK

Sometimes simple materials can be turned into a useful device. Watch how paper cups, a dowel, and straws become a fun machine!

What You Need:

scissors

paper

straw

glue or tape

2 paper cups or cardboard tubes

hole punch

dowel or craft stick

pipe cleaner

What You Do:

1 Cut two identical people shapes out of paper. Cut a straw in half and glue or tape it between the two paper shapes.

2 Punch two holes across from each other in each cup. Slide one end of the dowel through one cup's holes.

3 Slide the straw with the paper shapes onto the dowel. Slide the remaining dowel end through the other cup's holes.

4 Bend a pipe cleaner in a loop and connect it to the dowel on each side of the paper shape.

5 Glue the other straw half to one end of the dowel to make a crank.

6 Turn the crank and watch Jack jump!

TIP If Jack moves with the jump rope, reposition the jump rope and make sure the paper shapes are balanced.

BRIDGE IT!

It can take a team of engineers years to design and build a new bridge. But you can build one in just 10 minutes!

What You Need:

6 pencils, 4 sharpened

6 rubber bands

cardboard, about 6x4 inches (15x10 cm)

tape or glue

8–10 craft sticks

What You Do:

1 Cross the eraser ends of two sharpened pencils to make a V. Wrap a rubber band around the ends.

2 Repeat step 1 with two other sharpened pencils. Then stand up each pencil V on a long end of the cardboard. Stick the sharpened end of each pencil into the cardboard to keep in place.

3 Tape or glue the craft sticks together to make a bridge deck. Tape two more pencils to the long edges, leaving each end sticking out past the sticks.

4 Place the bridge deck between the Vs. Wrap rubber bands where the pencils meet.

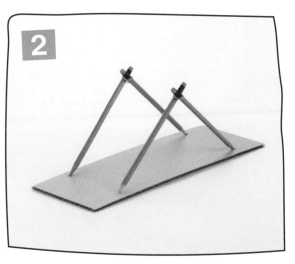

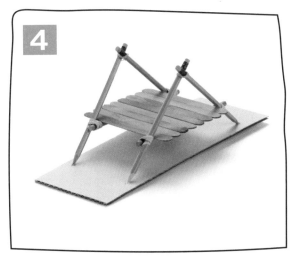

TIP Test it out! Try putting cars or building blocks on the bridge. How much weight can it hold? How could you redesign the bridge to make it stronger?

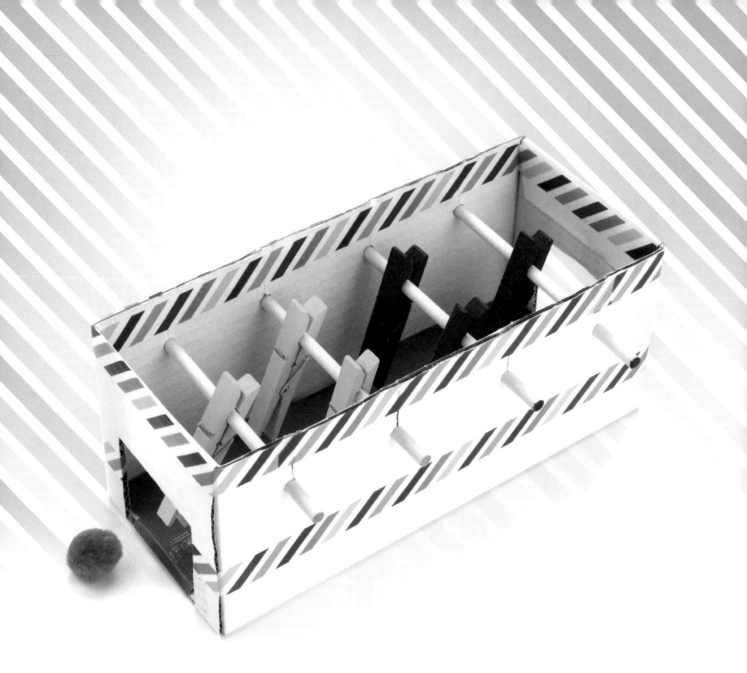

KICK BALL

Engineering isn't all about work! Simple machines like levers make work easier. Clothespins act as levers in this fun game. A twist of a dowel moves a lever, and the lever pushes the load (a ball).

What You Need:

scissors or craft knife

cardboard box, shoebox size

6 regular-sized clothespins, two colors

hole punch

4 dowels

washi tape or markers

pom-pom

What You Do:

1 Cut a square out of each end of a box to make goals.

2 Clip two clothespins of one color to a dowel. Then clip one clothespin of the same color to the middle of another dowel. Repeat with the other color clothespins.

3 Set the dowels on the top edge of the box, spacing them evenly. From the bottom of the box, draw a 2 ½-inch (6.4-cm) line up toward each dowel end. Then punch a hole at each line's end.

4 Slide the dowels into the holes. The clothespins should hang above the bottom of the box without touching it.

5 Decorate the bottom and sides of the box with tape or markers.

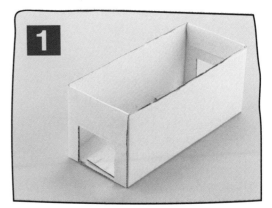

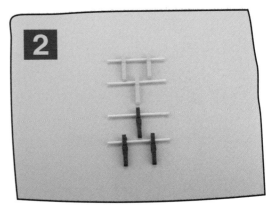

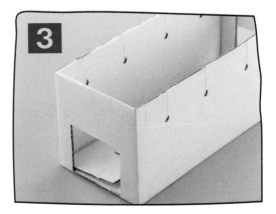

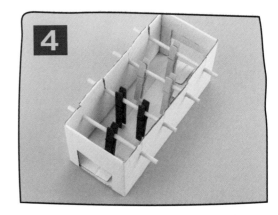

TIP When you're ready to play, add a pom-pom, twist the dowels, and watch the levers hit the pom-pom into a goal. Score!

ROOSTER RACER

Repurpose pool noodles! Build rooster racers with your friends and see which one reaches the finish line first.

What You Need:

scissors or craft knife

pool noodles

round toothpicks

straw

craft stick

glue or tape

What You Do:

1 Slice or cut pool noodles into rooster shapes.

2 Use four circles to make wheels. Stuff an extra piece of noodle into the center hole of each of the wheels. Stick a toothpick into the center of two wheels.

3 Cut two 1-inch (2.5-cm) pieces of straw. Slide one straw piece onto each toothpick. Stick the toothpicks into the other two wheels.

4 Glue or tape a craft stick to the straws. The piece will look like a skateboard with large wheels.

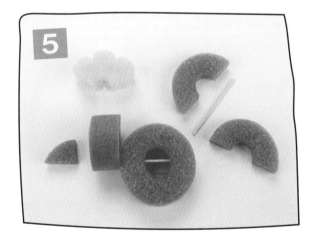

5 Connect different shapes and sizes of noodle slices with toothpicks to make a rooster. Glue it to the craft stick.

TIP You can connect and build anything with pool noodle slices and toothpicks. Try building a tower or bridge!

FLYING FISH

If roosters can race, then fish can fly! Design your own zip line and watch gravity at work. Get zipping!

What You Need:

marker
cardboard
scissors
2 paper clips
string
chairs
duct tape

What You Do:

1 Draw an outline of a fish about as big as your hand on cardboard. Cut it out.

2 Unbend the paper clips to make two S shapes.

3 Duct tape the paper clips to the fish, then cover the entire fish with tape as well.

4 Draw a funny face on your fish.

5 Bend the top of the paper clips outward.

6 Tie a string between two chairs of different heights. Hang the fish on the string at the high end. Push the fish and watch it fly!

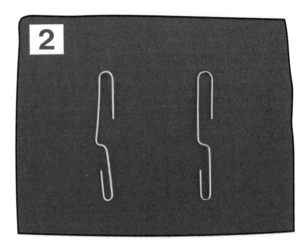

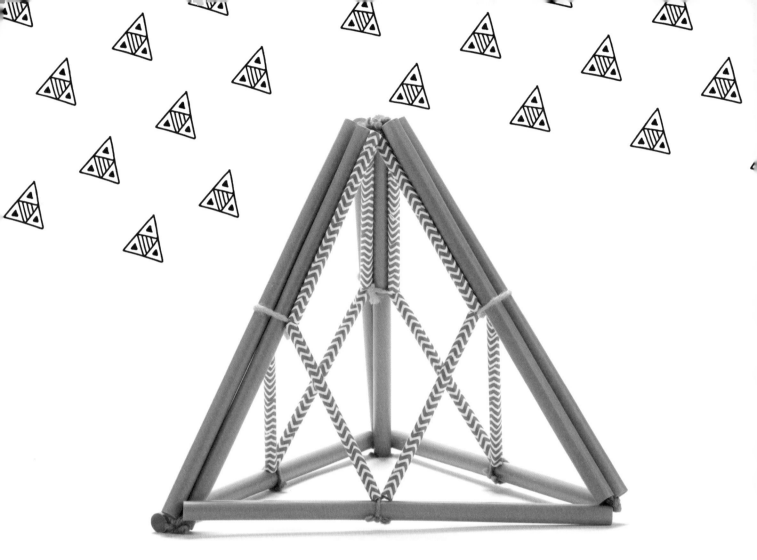

TRIANGLE CRAZE

Triangles are a common shape used in architecture.
They add stability and strength to a structure.
Experiment with this important shape
by building this pyramid of triangles!

What You Do:

1 Thread yarn through three straws. Tie the ends of yarn together to make a triangle. Repeat to make two more triangles.

2 Cut two other straws in half. Thread yarn through the four pieces and tie the ends to make a diamond. Repeat to make two more diamonds.

3 Form a pyramid with the triangles. Tie a diamond to the top, sides, and bottom of the pyramid on each side.

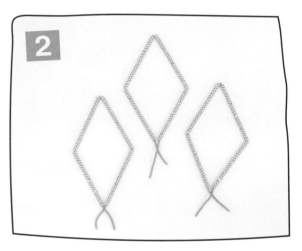

TIP Try working with friends to build a larger structure. Watch how high your pyramid stacks can get!

BALANCE IT!

Engineering meets modern art in this simple
sculpture. How high can you go? Can you balance it?

What You Need:

table tennis balls
large craft sticks
poster putty or clay
cardboard tube

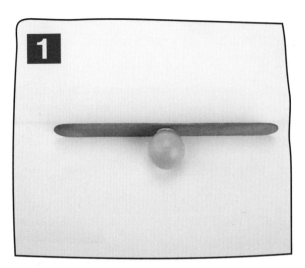

What You Do:

1 Attach table tennis balls to craft sticks with putty.

2 Stack the sticks and balls on top of each other.

3 Add a cardboard tube beneath the bottom stick. Adjust the putty to make the sculpture balance.

TIP For best results, make sure your working surface is flat. For an extra challenge, try adding more balls, sticks, and tubes to the structure.

81

ROLL IT UP!

Even engineers need to improve their designs to make sure buildings will not collapse. Test the strength of these simple paper tubes. How much weight can they hold before they collapse? Try it and find out!

What You Need:

6 pieces of paper

tape

different "loads" (books, toy cars, building blocks)

What You Do:

1 Roll each piece of paper into a tube. Tape along the long edge.

2 Stand the tubes together and place a notebook or two on top.

3 Set toys or building blocks on top of the notebooks.

1

2

TIP Try adding different loads on top of the notebooks. How much can the tubes hold before they crumple from the weight? For even more challenges, try changing the number of tubes. How many tubes are needed to hold one textbook?

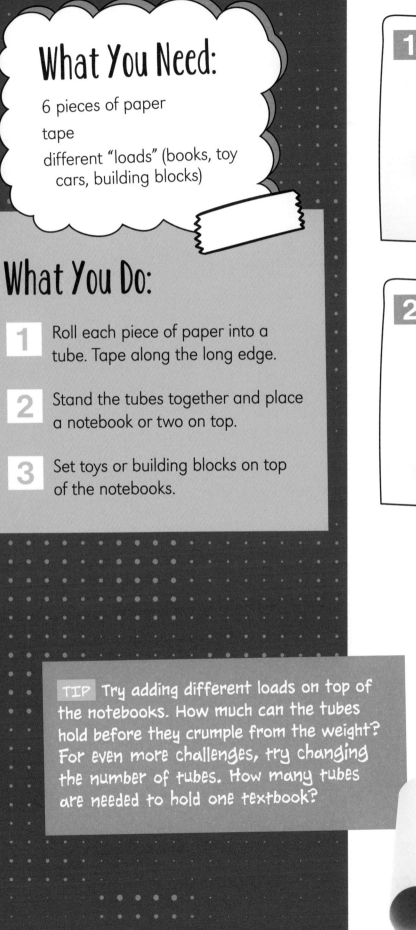

WINCH WAY?

Pulleys and winches are simple machines that make work easier. See for yourself. Winch way will it go?

What You Need:

cardboard tube

craft paper or washi tape

2 mini clothespins

string or yarn, about 8 inches
  (20 cm) long

lollipop stick

scissors

small bucket or cup with handle

What You Do:

1 Cover a cardboard tube with craft paper or washi tape.

2 Clip the clothespins to the stick. The stick should rest loosely in the holes of the clothespin.

3 Tie one end of the string to the center of the stick. Tie the other end to the handle of the bucket.

4 Glue the clothespins to the inside of one end of the cardboard tube.

5 Twist the stick to make the bucket go up and down.

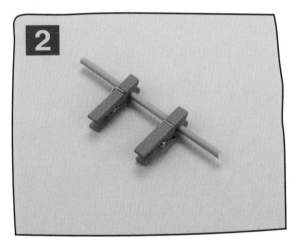

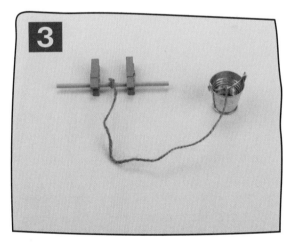

MARBLE A-MAZE-ING

Make your next marble run portable!
It will be a-maze-ing!

What You Need:

cardboard lid or shallow box

craft sticks

wooden blocks

tape, washi tape, or glue

clear plastic place mat
    or sheet

scissors

marble

What You Do:

1 Set the craft sticks and wooden blocks in the lid. Plan where you want them to go. Tape them to the box to test your maze.

2 Once you have a design you like, glue the sticks and blocks to the lid.

3 Put a marble in the maze. Lay the plastic on top of the lid and cut it to fit.

4 Tape the plastic piece to the lid. Decorate the sides with more tape.

5 Move the box back and forth to try and get the marble through the maze.

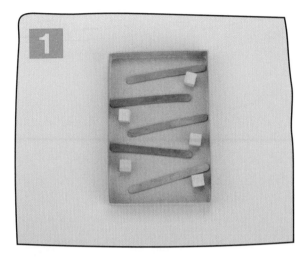

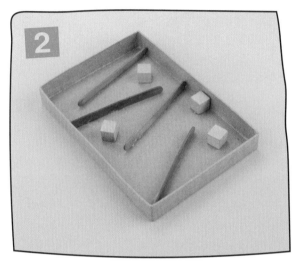

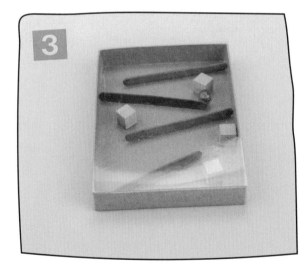

MAGNET PLANE

Combine wings, wheels, and a magnet
to create a simple airplane. Use a bar
magnet to watch your plane really move!

What You Need:

9 large craft sticks

hot glue gun or duct tape

plastic wheels or bottle caps

straw

2 toothpicks

scissors

craft magnet

bar magnet

What You Do:

1 Stack seven craft sticks on top of each other to look like an airplane. Glue or tape them together.

2 Cut the remaining two craft sticks in half. Cut one of the sticks in half again. Glue the pieces to the plane to make wings and a tail.

3 Cut two small pieces of straw, shorter than the toothpicks. Slide the straws onto the toothpicks.

4 Connect a wheel to each end of the toothpicks. Glue the straw pieces to the bottom of the plane.

5 Glue a craft magnet to the back of the plane. Hold a bar magnet near the back of the plane to repel the craft magnet. Watch your plane move!

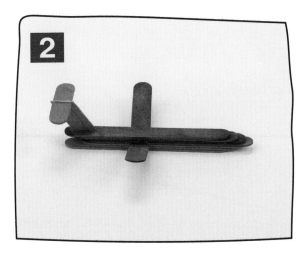

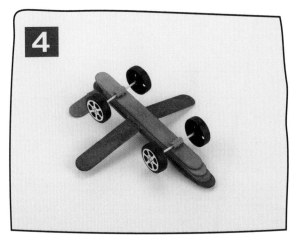

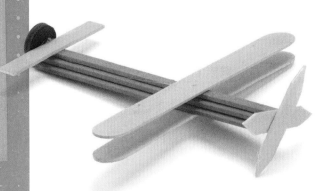

FLIP-BOOK

What makes you smile? A funny-face flip-book
should do the trick. Improve your drawing skills
and have fun at the same time.

What You Need:

photographs of faces, all same size
notebook
glue
scissors
marker

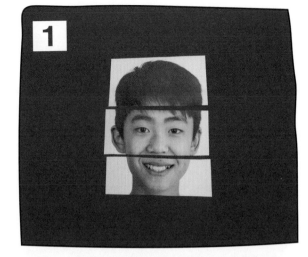

What You Do:

1 Make sure all photos are facing up. Stack them on top of each other. Then cut the stack horizontally into three equal pieces.

2 Glue three strips to each notebook page. Cut the paper to match the strips.

3 Flip the strips back and forth to make mixed-up faces.

TIP Take pictures of your friends, family, pets, and even yourself to use in this project. Or cut pictures out of magazines or old books. Draw accessories, such as glasses, with markers.

NINJA CLIMBER

Only have one piece of paper? No problem!
With a few simple folds, you can make a ninja
that magically climbs up and down.

What You Need:

paper, 2½ x 11 inches
   (6 x 28 cm)

marker

scissors

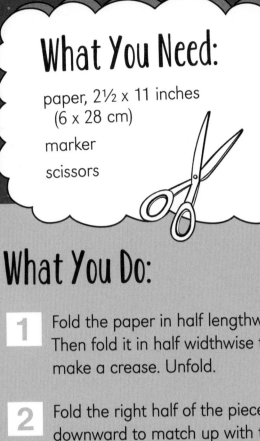

What You Do:

1 Fold the paper in half lengthwise. Then fold it in half widthwise to make a crease. Unfold.

2 Fold the right half of the piece downward to match up with the vertical center crease you made in step 1.

3 Repeat step 2 on the left side. Unfold both sides.

4 Using your right index finger, squash the right side of the piece along the crease. Repeat on the left side.

5 Flip the paper over. Draw a ninja face on the triangle tip. Cut off the tip.

6 Place your ninja between the two pieces of paper. Move one side of the climber up while you move the other side down.

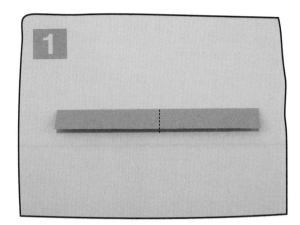

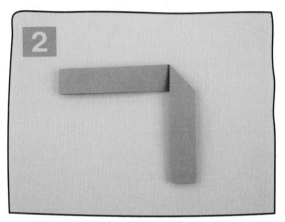

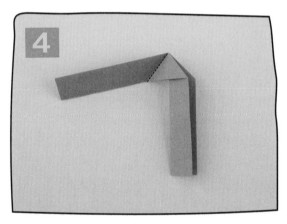

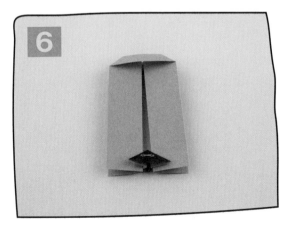

DREAM CATCHER

Roll up some old book or magazine pages
to make beads to hang from a simple paper plate.
Place this easy dream catcher in your room
to remind you to follow your dreams!

What You Need:

paper plates, different colors

pencil

scissors

yarn

tape

strips of paper (optional)

What You Do:

1 Draw a star or your favorite shape in the middle of a paper plate. Cut it out. Then poke holes with a pencil around the cutout.

2 Tape the end of a piece of yarn to make it pointy, like a needle. From the back of the plate, pull the "needle" and yarn through one hole, leaving a bit of yarn to tape to the back.

3 Then sew in and out of the holes. Tape the needle end to the back of the plate when finished. Tape a larger plate to the back of the first plate.

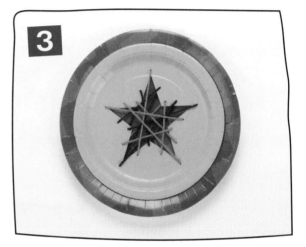

TIP If you have more time, roll paper with a pencil to make beads. String the beads onto yarn. Then tape the yarn pieces to the back of the plate so they hang from the bottom.

PICTURE IT

Got paper? Roll it up and turn those
simple paper tubes into a stunning picture frame.
Just add your favorite photo!

What You Need:

scissors

old magazines, book pages, or patterned paper

glue

cardboard, cut to frame your picture

What You Do:

1 Cut strips of old magazines or scrap paper pages. You can make them any size you wish.

2 Roll the strips into tubes. Glue or tape the edges.

3 Put a favorite picture, or draw your own, in the middle of the frame.

4 Glue the tubes around the outside of the frame. Be careful not to glue them onto the picture.

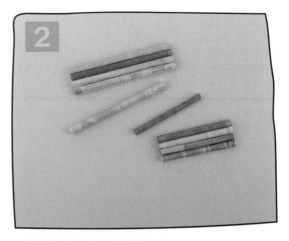

PAPER CHAIN BRACELET

Decorate your wrist with this easy paper chain bracelet. You don't even need tape or glue!

What You Need:

scissors

about 20 paper strips, 4¼ inches x ½ inch (10.8 x 1.3 cm) each

ruler

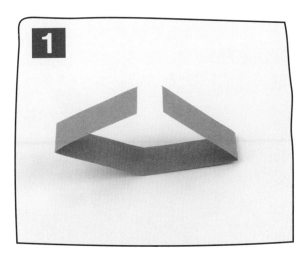

What You Do:

1 Fold one strip of paper in half, then unfold it. Fold the right edge of the strip into the middle line. Then fold the left side to the middle.

2 Fold the strip in half again. Set aside. Repeat steps 1 and 2 with the rest of the strips.

3 Slide the folded edges of one strip into the slits of another folded strip. Push it all the way through to fit snugly.

4 Continue adding more strips to create a zigzag pattern. Slide the two ends of the first and last strips of paper together to finish it.

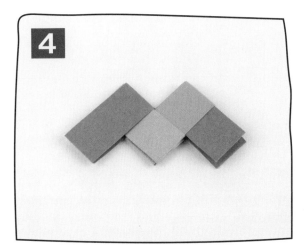

TIP Want to make a necklace or chain? Just make more strips of paper, fold them, and slide them on!

HANGING 3-D SCULPTURE

Take paper to a whole new dimension with an epic 3-D sculpture! Hang it in your locker or bedroom to add some fun flair.

What You Need:

scissors

card stock, different colors

What You Do:

1 Cut out a large shape from card stock. Start with a circle or square. This will be your center shape. Set aside.

2 Cut out several smaller versions of the same shape from card stock. Fold each shape in half.

3 In the center of the folded edge of each of the shapes, cut a slit. Make sure you don't cut all the way to the edges.

4 Open each shape. Using the cut slits, slide each shape, largest to smallest, onto the center shape.

5 Add more shapes to build a large 3-D shape.

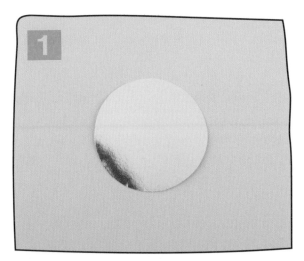

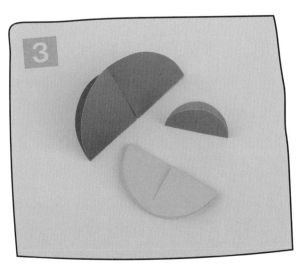

HIGH-FIVE BOOKMARK

Need a hand keeping a page marked in that book you're reading? Never fear! The high-five bookmark is here!

What You Need:

pencil
paper
scissors
glue or tape
paper clip

What You Do:

1 Trace your own hand or draw a small hand on a piece of paper. Cut it out.

2 Cut thin strips of paper. Use a pencil tip to coil the strips.

3 Glue the coiled strips of paper to the hand.

4 Glue or tape a paper clip to the back of the hand to make a bookmark.

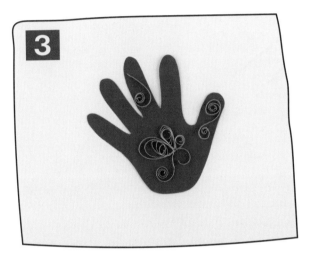

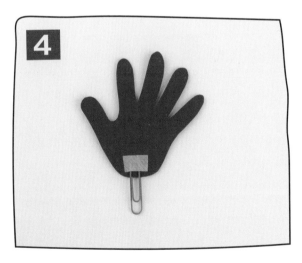

THUMBTACK LANTERN

Light up your life with a colorful lantern.
On a cloudy day, it will bring the sunshine indoors!

What You Need:

pencil
colored paper or paper tube
thumbtack or pin
tape
battery-powered candle

What You Do:

1 Lightly draw a pattern on a piece of paper.

2 Use a thumbtack to poke holes around the lines of the design. Erase any visible pencil marks.

3 Roll the paper into a tube and tape it together.

4 Set the tube over a battery-powered candle to make a lantern.

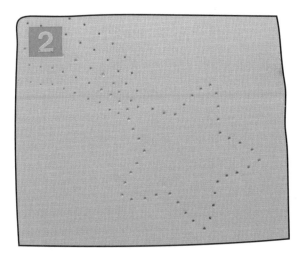

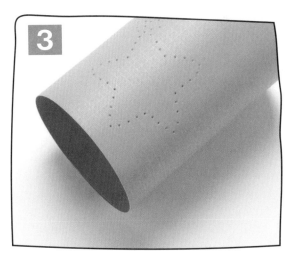

LAUNCH IT!

Draw or fold your own rocket and watch
it soar through the air. Launch away!

What You Need:

markers

card stock

scissors

paper clip

hole punch

hammer

scrap wood or wooden
building block

2 nails

rubber band

What You Do:

1 Draw a rocket on card stock and cut it out. Decorate it with markers.

2 Unfold a paper clip to make an S. Bend one of the hooks to the side.

3 Use a hole punch to make two holes in the body of the rocket. Thread one loop of the paper clip through the holes.

4 Pound a nail near each end of a small wooden block. Stretch a rubber band around the nails.

5 Attach the other loop of the paper clip to the rubber band. Pull the rocket back and let go. Liftoff!

TIP If you don't have scrap wood, just flip a chair over, stretch a rubber band across two of the chair legs, and launch your rockets.

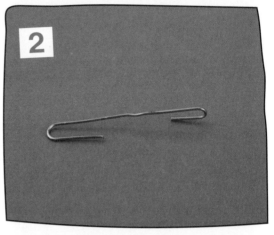

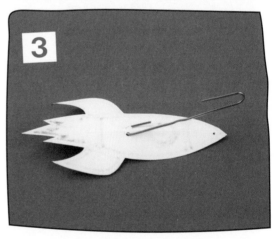

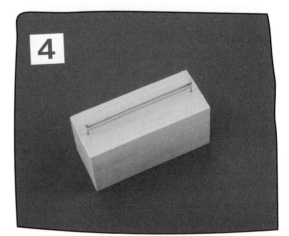

LOCKER MAGNET MESSAGES

You don't need a cell phone to send messages.
Surprise your friends with text message magnets!

What You Need:

scissors
dry-erase contact paper
paper and cardboard
glue
dry-erase markers
craft magnets

What You Do:

1 Cut text bubbles out of dry-erase contact paper.

2 Cut cell phone screen shapes out of paper and cardboard. Glue them together.

3 Stick the text message bubbles to the paper.

4 Glue magnets on the back.

5 Use dry-erase markers to write some fun messages to a friend.

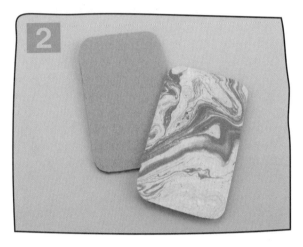

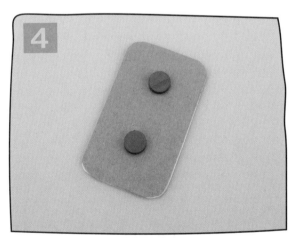

TIP Use a magnet to attach the dry-erase pen to your friend's locker. Your friend will be able to reply to you!

PAPER PET

What's your favorite pet? Don't have a pet?
Make your own paper pet to enjoy.

What You Need:

scissors

card stock or cardboard

markers

paper

What You Do:

1 Cut a pet shape out of card stock or cardboard.

2 Use markers to add some color to your pet.

3 Use paper and markers to make outfits, hats, scarves, sunglasses, or other accessories for your pet.

TIP Change the clothes on your pets to match what you are wearing. Or make uniforms for your favorite sports teams.

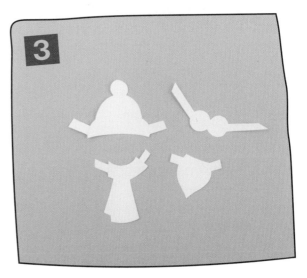

PAPER SPINNER

Feeling fidgety? This simple paper spinner should do the trick. Spin up some fun!

What You Need:

- pencil
- paper
- markers
- cardboard
- scissors
- glue stick
- string

What You Do:

1 Draw two circles of the same size on paper. Use markers to color or draw patterns on the circles. Cut them out.

2 Set one of the paper circles on top of a piece of cardboard. Trace it, then cut out the cardboard circle.

3 Glue a paper circle on each side of the cardboard circle.

4 Poke two holes through the center of the circle with the pencil tip.

5 Cut a piece of string about 30 inches (76 cm) long. Thread the string through both holes, then tie the ends in a knot.

6 With a loop of string in each hand, wind the spinner, then pull. Watch it spin!

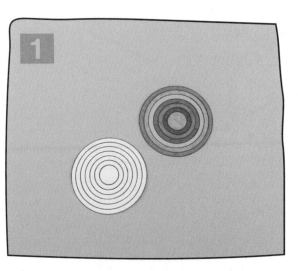

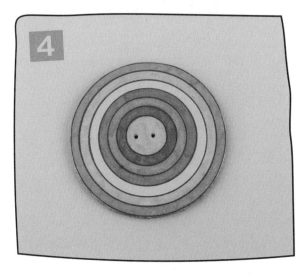

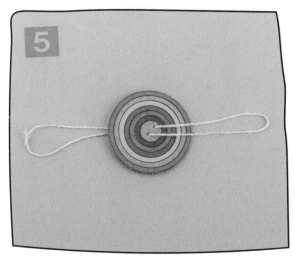

A FORTUNATE COOKIE

Show your friends that you care about them.
Fold these paper fortune cookies and write
encouraging notes inside.

What You Need:

scissors

paper

glue or tape

string and paper punch (optional)

What You Do:

1 Cut a circle out of paper about 4½ inches (11.4 cm) across.

2 From the paper scraps, cut a thin rectangle. Write a fortune on the strip.

3 Lay the fortune on top of the circle. Roll the circle into a tube and tape it shut.

4 Press down on the folded circle's center, then make a crease.

5 Pinch down the sides of the folded circle. Add glue or tape inside the crease.

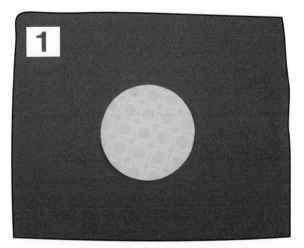

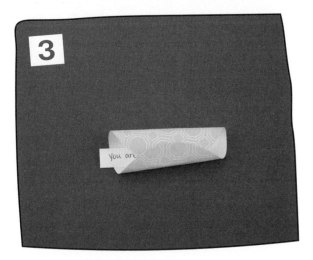

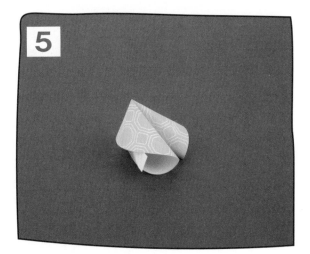

TIP String a bunch of fortune cookies together to make a garland or decoration for your room.

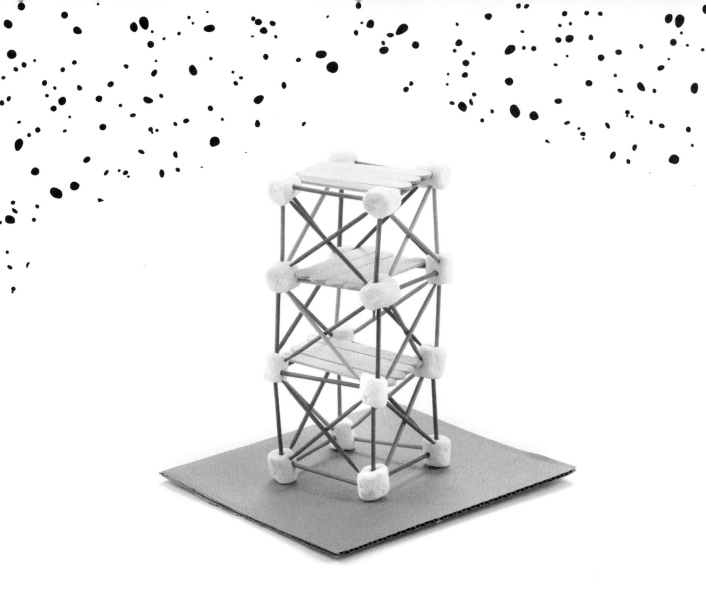

EARTHQUAKE PROOF?

Can you build a structure that stands strong during a pretend earthquake? Experiment with different designs. What works the best?

What You Need:

40 toothpicks
16 mini marshmallows
glue
12 mini craft sticks
cardboard

What You Do:

1 Form a square with 4 toothpicks and 4 marshmallows.

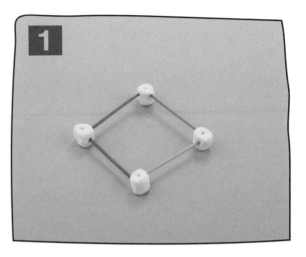

2 Repeat step 1 to make a second square. Using the two squares and four more toothpicks, form a cube.

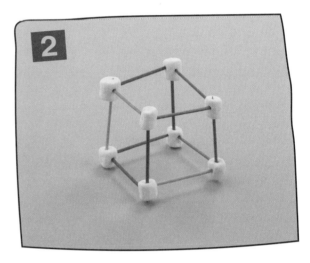

3 Use 8 more toothpicks to make an X in each side of the cube. The Xs will add support.

4 Glue 4 mini craft sticks together to make a platform. Place the platform on top of the cube.

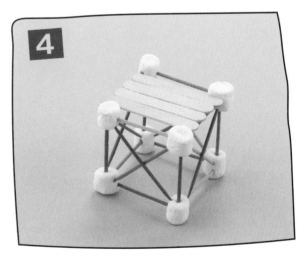

5 Build two more cubes and platforms on top of the first cube. Then place the structure on a large piece of cardboard.

6 Slide the cardboard back and forth quickly. What happens?

7 Remove some of the structure's supports, then slide the cardboard back and forth again. What happens?

MAKE IT RAIN

Meteorologists study the weather, including cloud formation and rainfall. Bring the outdoors in to make and study your own rain-making cloud!

What You Need:

jar
water
shaving cream
eye dropper
food coloring

What You Do:

1 Fill a jar or glass with water. Add a dollop of shaving cream to the top.

2 Add 3 or 4 drops of food coloring on top of the shaving cream.

3 Using an eye dropper, drop water on top of the shaving cream, one drop at a time.

4 How many drops of water does it take before the cream cloud starts to "rain"?

TIP Experiment with dropping different liquids, such as orange juice or corn syrup. Try whipped topping for the clouds.

FOSSIL FUN

Fossils are the bones, shells, or other remains
of plants and animals preserved as rocks.
They can take millions of years to form.
But you can make your own "fossils" today
out of plants, rocks, and even toys.

What You Need:

1 cup (227 g) flour

½ cup (114 g) salt

¼ cup (60 mL) warm water

food coloring

bowl

cutting board or wax paper

cookie cutter

skewer

toys, rocks, plants, leaves

string or yarn (optional)

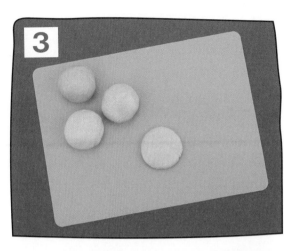

What You Do:

1 Mix the flour, salt, and water in a bowl. To make colored dough, add food coloring to the warm water before adding to the dry ingredients.

2 Squish the mixture with your hands until it is smooth.

3 Press balls of dough onto a cutting board or piece of wax paper. Use a cookie cutter to make a shape.

4 Press a toy into the dough to make a footprint or impression. Or press a rock into the dough.

5 Use a skewer to poke a hole in the top of the shape.

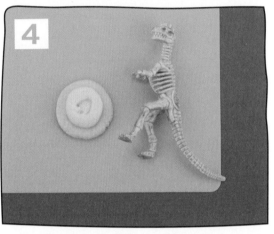

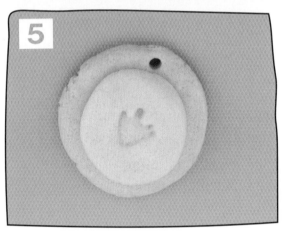

TIP Let the dough dry overnight, if you can. When dry, thread string or yarn through the hole at the top. Use your fossil as a necklace or zipper pull.

CELL CARD

Scientists and artists both teach us about the world.
Turn your favorite science topic into an
artistic and fun greeting card!

What You Need:

pencil

card stock

scissors

straws in blues and greens

glue

felt or craft foam, washi tape, markers (optional)

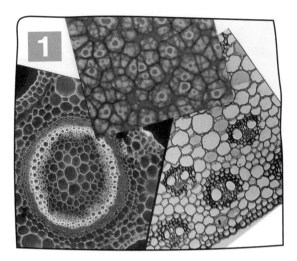

What You Do:

1. Look up a plant cell image on the internet.

2. Draw the outline of a plant cell on a folded piece of card stock.

3. Cut straws into small pieces.

4. Glue the straw pieces to the front of the card to make a plant cell.

TIP Make an animal cell instead! Use felt or craft foam, washi tape, markers, and straws to represent the parts of the cell.

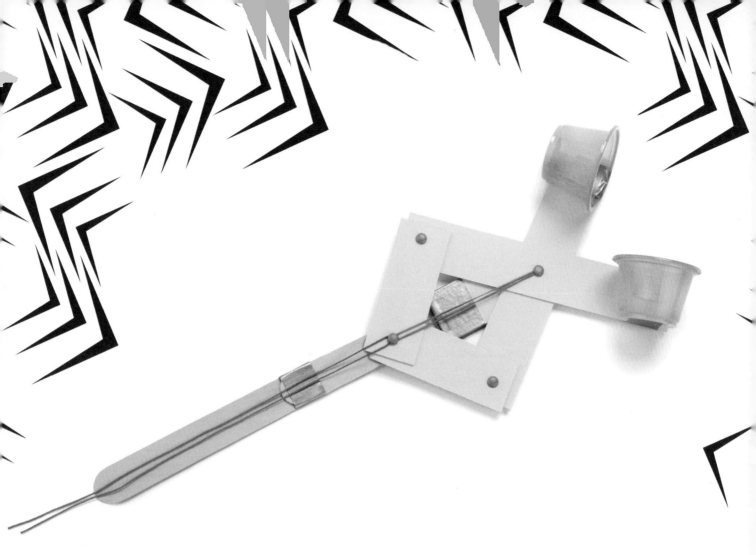

GRABBER CLAW

Can you think and design like an engineer?
Create your own grabber claw and watch
it do work for you!

What You Need:

duct tape

2 large craft sticks

scissors

3 cardboard pieces,
1½ x 4 inches
(4 x 10 cm)

2 cardboard pieces,
1½ x 8 inches
(4 x 20 cm)

4 brad fasteners

rubber band

string, 24 inches
(61 cm) long

2 small plastic
cups

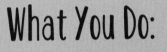

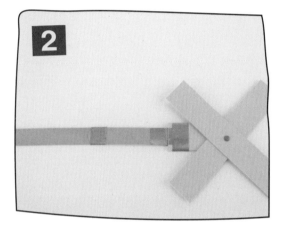

What You Do:

1 Tape the craft sticks together, end to end. Tape one of the shorter pieces of cardboard to one end.

2 Make an X with the two long pieces of cardboard. Poke a brad fastener through the middle. Then poke it through the cardboard piece on the end of the craft stick from step 1.

3 At the bottom of the X, attach the remaining cardboard pieces with three more brad fasteners.

4 Attach a rubber band around the two middle brad fasteners.

5 Loop the string around the bottom fastener and let the ends hang down the handle.

6 Tape a plastic cup to each end of the grabber. Pull on the string to move the claw.

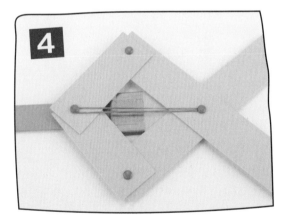

LASER POINTER

Learn how simple circuits and switches work by making your own laser pointer. It will be the brightest part of your day!

What You Need:

copper tape
craft stick
button battery CR2032
binder clip
3–3.2V LED bulb

What You Do:

1 Stick copper tape down on one side of a craft stick.

2 Set a button battery on one end of the stick. It should be positive (+) side down and touching the copper tape.

3 Attach the battery to the stick with a binder clip. Then flip one metal arm down onto the battery.

4 On the back of the stick, add another strip of copper tape. Flip down the other metal clip arm so it touches the tape.

5 Slide an LED bulb over the other end of the stick. The long leg should be on the side with the battery. The short leg should be touching the copper tape on the back.

6 If the LED doesn't light up, check the connections and try again. Flip the metal arm away from the battery to turn off the light.

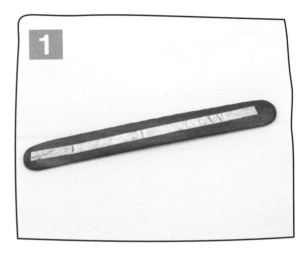

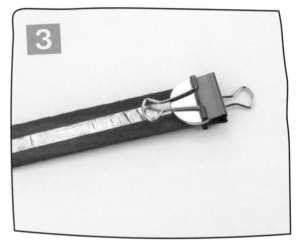

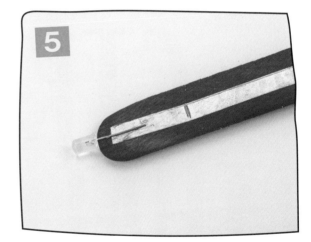

TIP Copper and foil are conductors of electricity. If you don't have copper tape, you can try using foil.

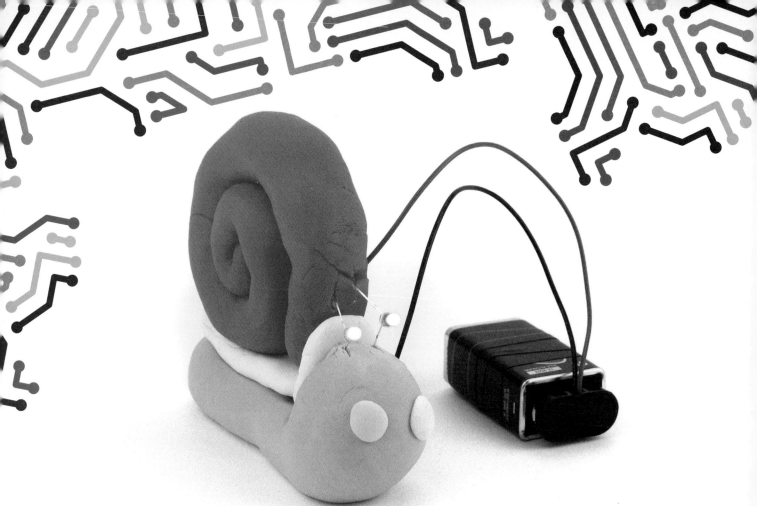

CIRCUITS THAT SQUISH

Salt is a good conductor of electricity.
Try making these circuits that squish
and light up before your eyes!

What You Need:

play dough

modeling clay

2 9V LED bulbs

9V battery with holder
and wire leads

What You Do:

1 Roll play dough into a long piece and coil it to look like a snail's shell.

2 Form a second piece of play dough into the snail's head and body. Add eyes.

3 Put a piece of modeling clay between the two dough shapes to hold them together.

4 Stick the red wire into the snail's shell. Stick the black wire into the snail's body.

5 Open the legs of an LED bulb. Stick the long leg into the snail's shell. Stick the other leg into the snail's body. The LED bulb will light up!

6 Repeat Step 5 with the second LED bulb.

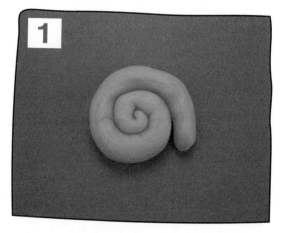

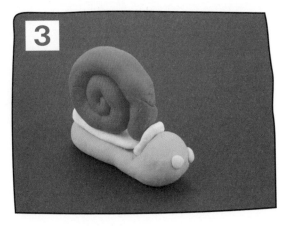

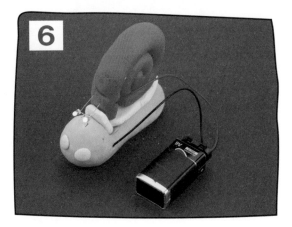

TIP If your bulb doesn't light up right away, check your connections and try again. The salt in the dough acts as a conductor of electricity. The modeling clay acts as an insulator.

GLITTER PUTTY

Chemicals react and change molecules into something new. Watch how simple chemicals change into gooey putty right before your eyes!

What You Need:

¼ cup (60 mL) shampoo
  or bodywash

1 cup (227 g) cornstarch

bowl

spoon

4-7 teaspoons (20-35 mL) water

glitter and food coloring

What You Do:

1 Mix the shampoo and cornstarch in a bowl until it is crumbly.

2 Mix in the water, one teaspoon at a time, until the mixture is gooey. Add food coloring and glitter.

3 Kneed the mixture with your hands for 5 minutes until it is smooth.

4 Keep your slime in a covered container. Refresh it with a spoonful of water if it gets dry.

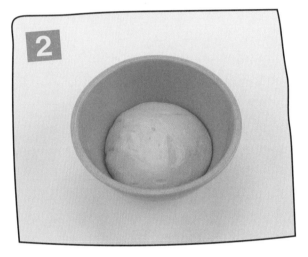

TIP Use the thickest shampoo you can find. Or you can use equal amounts of shampoo and your favorite body wash. You can even use lotion instead. All of these ingredients are safe and smell great too.

LEMON-LIME LAVA

Acids, like vinegar and citrus fruits, make carbon dioxide when they react with bases, like baking soda. Test the reactive properties of limes, lemons, oranges, and grapefruit with this experiment. Which fruit has the biggest reaction?

What You Need:

limes, lemons, oranges, and grapefruits

knife

plastic cups or plates

baking soda

food coloring

dish soap

½ cup (125 mL) vinegar

spoon

What You Do:

1 Ask an adult to cut a lime and lemon in half. Squeeze the fruits with your hands and pour the juice into a cup or container.

2 Add a spoonful of baking soda, 3-4 drops of food coloring, and a drop of dish soap to the middle of each fruit.

3 Set the lemon and lime halves on top of each other on a small plate. Pour the lemon and lime juice down the fruit.

4 Then pour the vinegar onto the fruit. What happens?

5 Repeat the experiment with other fruits. Record your observations.

MOVING STARS

Water can change the shape and form of other natural objects, such as wood. Wood absorbs water because it is porous. Watch these simple toothpick stars move with a few drops of water!

What You Need:

5 toothpicks

water

eye dropper

What You Do:

1 Bend each of the toothpicks in half without breaking them.

2 Lay the toothpicks in a star shape.

3 Using the eye dropper, drip 10 drops of water in the center of the star.

4 Watch as your star starts to move!

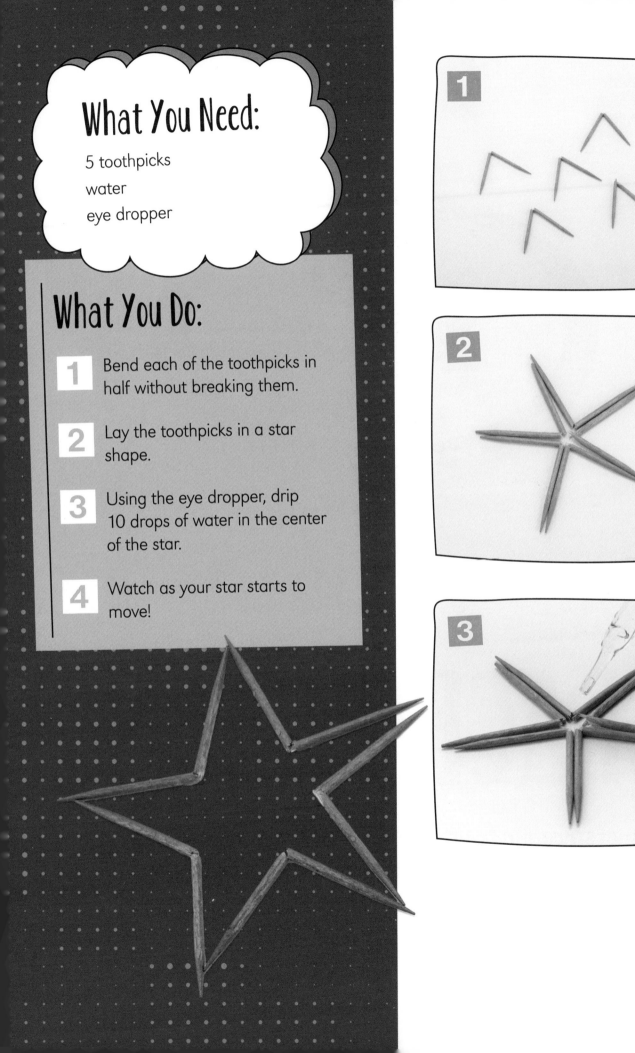

SPACE ROCKS!

Planets are made up of solids, gases, and liquids that are always changing. You can't travel to another planet, but you can make these fuzzy space rocks!

What You Need:

spoon

bowl

1 tablespoon (15 g) baking soda

1 tablespoon (15 g) salt

1 tablespoon (15 g) cornstarch

food coloring or paint

1 tablespoon (15 mL) water

glitter

plastic containers/zip-top bags or
    paper cups

vinegar

What You Do:

1 Mix the baking soda, salt, and cornstarch together in a bowl.

2 Add the water, two drops of food coloring, and some glitter. Mix with the dry ingredients.

3 Using your hands, form the mixture into balls.

4 Set the "rocks" in a cup or container. Pour 1 teaspoon of vinegar over the rocks. What happens?

5 You can repeat the experiment at different temperatures. Use the freezer as a "cold planet." With frozen rocks, does the reaction change?

TIP If the mixture is too wet to form the rocks, just sprinkle in more soda. You can let the rocks dry overnight if you have more time. The experiment will still work the next day.

SAY WHAT?

Sound travels in waves. Build this simple flute to test how sound waves travel through materials.

What You Need:

- 2 large craft sticks/ice pop sticks
- 4 rubber bands
- washi tape
- scissors
- 5 or more straws, cut to different lengths

What You Do:

1 Stretch two rubber bands across each craft stick. Tape the ends in place.

2 Weave each end of the shortest straw through the rubber bands on each stick.

3 Going shortest to longest, repeat step 2 with the remaining straws, but alternate the weave with each straw.

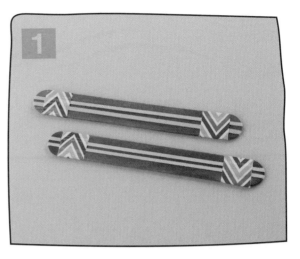

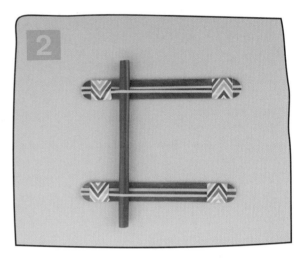

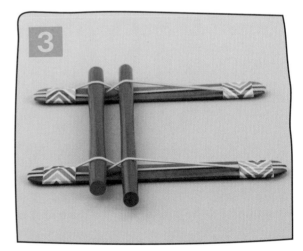

TIP Blow air through each straw. Do you hear a different pitch from each one? Does a longer straw make a higher or lower pitch?

USE THOSE LUNGS!

Like your heart, your lungs help move oxygen through your body. Taking deep breaths can even help us calm down when we are stressed. Learn how your lungs work with this simple project.

What You Need:

2 bendy straws

1 large straw

2 rubber bands

2 small balloons

plastic bottle with cap

craft knife or scissors

1 large balloon

poster board, cardboard,
   washi tape (optional)

What You Do:

1 Slide the two bendy straws into the larger straw. Leave the bendy ends hanging out.

2 Use a rubber band to attach a balloon to each bendy straw. Blow into the straw to make sure it is airtight.

3 Ask an adult to cut off the bottom of the bottle and use a craft knife to poke a hole in the cap.

4 Slide the large straw with balloons through the bottom of the bottle. Slide the end of the straw through the cap.

5 Cut a large balloon in half and tie the end. Stretch it over the bottom of the bottle.

6 Blow into the straw and watch the lungs fill with air.

1

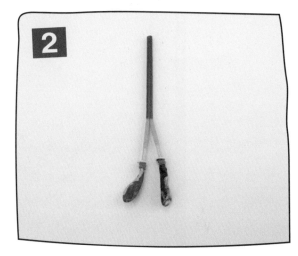

2

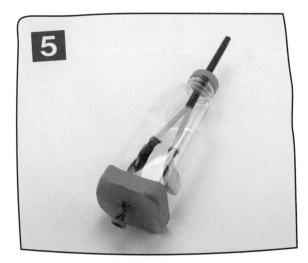

5

TIP The straws act like your bronchial tubes. The small balloons are like your air sacs, called alveoli. The large balloon acts like your diaphragm.

Folding **PAPER AIRPLANES** with **STEM**

For Beginners to Experts

30+ AWESOME PROJECTS!

by Marie Buckingham

Check out these other fun Capstone books, and you'll be busy for days!

Dabble Lab is published by Capstone Press, a Capstone imprint.
1710 Roe Crest Drive, North Mankato, Minnesota 56003
www.capstonepub.com

Library of Congress Cataloging-in-Publication data
is availableon the Library of Congress website.
ISBN 978-1-4966-8680-0 (paperback)
ISBN 978-1-4966-8682-4 (eBook PDF)

Summary: Got 10 minutes? Get making with quick, self-guided projects and activities that are sure to please and won't break the bank. From duct tape tablet holders and paper beads to bubbling lava cups, these fun projects will have kids making in no time.

Editorial Credits
Editor: Shelly Lyons; Designer: Tracy McCabe;
Media Researcher: Tracy Cummins; Production Specialist: Katy LaVigne;
Project Production: Marcy Morin

Photo Credits
All photographs by Capstone: Karon Dubke

Design Elements
Shutterstock: Abra Cadabraaa, AllNikArt, ArtMari, Aygun Ali, best_vector, BewWanchai, Bimbim, Bjoern Wylezich, briddy, casejustin, DarkPlatypus, Designer things, Dr Project, drpnncpptak, eler, Epine, Evgeniya Pautova, Good Genie, H Art, hchjjl, il67, IrinaKrivoruchko, Kalinin Ilya, KannaA, Katata, keport, Kolonko, Maaike Boot, Maria Konstantinova, mila kad, Minur, newelle, Ninya Pavlova, ntnt, oksanka007, olllikeballoon, Piotr Urakau, Primsky, Redcollegiya, Sergey Edentod, sergio34, Shorena Tedliashvili, Silver Kitten, Smiling Fox, sollia, Sooa, StockSmartStart, strizh, Tanya Sun, Tiwat K, Tukang Desain, unpict, Valentain Jevee, Yes - Royalty Free, Yuliia Bahniuk, Zebra Finch

Printed and bound in China.
3322